MONOLOGUES for WOMEN

SUSAN POMERANCE

Dramaline® Publications

Dramaline Publications
36-851 Palm View Road
Rancho Mirage CA 92270
Phone 760/770-6076 Fax 760/770-4507
E-Mail: drama.line@gte.net
Web: dramaline.com

Library of Congress Cataloging-in-Publications Data

Pomerance, Susan.
    Monologues for women / Susan Pomerance.
        p. cm.
    ISBN 0-940669-49-8 (alk. paper)
    1. Monologues.   2. Acting.   3. Women—Drama.   I. Title.
PN2080 .P663 2001
812'.54—dc21   2001028559

Cover design by John Sabel

This book is printed on 55# Glatfelter acid-free paper, a paper that meets the requirements of the American Standard of Permanence of paper for printed library material.

CONTENTS

STELLA

Excessive remodeling has also remodeled her relationship.

Everything was cool. We were getting along fine. Then you have to go and bring in Lance, a refuge from *Architectual Digest.* Comes in like a swish of pastels. Mr. Know-it-All. Cons you into demoing the fireplace. The fireplace looked fine. There was nothing wrong with the fireplace. I tried to talk you out of it. But, oh no, Lance is an architect, a member of A. I. D. He's also a pompous, ego-inflated jerk. The Birkenstock sandals should tell you something. The guy's a throwback. He's lava lamps and phychedelic posters.

So, you listen to this dildo and he recommends monkeys with jackhammers. So, they come in on Monday morning at six o'clock with jackhammers and turn the place into Omaha Beach. And I'm supposed to be able to concentrate with all this dust and noise. I rewrote the same sentence ten times. You promised me peace and quiet when I moved in here. The perfect place to write while your away at the office, you said. Well . . . it all went from tranquility to bedlam in a matter of seconds. And this goddamn dust, this fine, white power is in everything: my computer, my clothes, books, hair, my eyes, mouth . . . God only knows what other orifices.

And then, you and Mr. Frank Lloyd Wright Jr., in your divine stupidity, decide to rip up the tile. So, the second wave of monkeys make a beachhead with chip hammers and scrapers and turn the place into a sandbox. This means I'm in the garage

1

trying my damnedest to meet a deadline for the *New Yorker*.
Now, I'm certainly no prima donna with a literary complex, but
I don't think I'm stretching it too much by saying that sitting in
the middle of a garage floor surrounded by oil drippings is not
the ideal catalyst for creativity.

And now you tell me you're going to replaster. Well, send
me an E-mail when you're finished.

I'm outta here.

*Old-fashioned ways which no longer apply to changed conditions are a
snare in which the feet of women have always become readily entalgled.*
—Jane Adams

LORAINE

Loraine experiences the frustrations of dealing with coroprate entities.

(On the phone.) Hello—God, I can't believe it. I almost gave up. I've been siting here for over ten minutes—Yes, ten minutes. Listening to bad electronic choruses of "Raindrops Keep Falling on My Head." Anyway, I'm calling about my claim—Yes . . . auto damage. This *is* Western Life, isn't it?—Okay, I'm calling about my claim. Your adjuster looked at my car three weeks ago—Loraine. Loraine Wells—555-375-2784—Claim Number? Hold on a sec. *(Beat.)* Claim number P329867200127HZ—No, not "Z," "P," as in Paul, as in Perry, as in Picture. *"P!"*—What? Okay, think slowly. "P," as in The Pope, 329867200127HZ.

You got that?—The adjuster's name? Hell, I don't know his name. All I know is, he was this weird looking little man with a pocket protector and green teeth—Bill Franklin? I see you've met him—A BMW—No no, not a VW, a BMW. Replace the VW with a BM—No, BM as in Bull Moose, as in Bowel Movement—I'm not being snippy, I'm just responding to three weeks of crazy back-and-forth over a minor fender dent. You'd think I was turning in a claim for major surgery—No, I'm not sick, it's just an expression. Forget it—What time of day? It's on the claim. 10:40 AM—No no, not BM. The car's a BM, the time of day is an AM—Look, I told you I don't drive a VW. Will you please stop it with the VW? I told you my car is a

BMW. It right there on the claim—What? You gotta be kidding—Once again, the numbert is "P," as in Pain-in-the-ass 329867200127HZ! No, my name is not Fred Epstein, it's Wells, Loraine Wells. Look, I don't care if Fred Epstein drives a VW. Frankly I don't give a bloody damn what Fred Epstein drives. Although, if he's dealing with Western Life, I'll pray for him. All I care about is getting a check so I can have my car repaired—It's in the mail? Why the didn't you say so?—I *did not* say "Z." I said *"P."* Hey, look. Nothing personal, but tell your company they can take their policy and shove it up their alphabet! (*Slams receiver.*)

A woman needs a man like a fish needs a bicycle.
                                        —Anonymous

DORIS

Frustrated by the state of her relationship, one that is unfulfilling and without commitment, Ellen lays it on the line.

I've given all I can. I just don't have any more. I love you. I've loved you since the night we met. And I've never stopped. But even the greatest love, the deepest love can only take so many rejections. Just what do you want, Harry, what is it that can satisfy you? Do you know? Or do you care to know? Is this a game you keep playing to keep from making a commitment? Is it some childish game of cat and mouse? Have you ever really grown up? Sometimes, when we're at our most intimate, I sense the greatest rejection. I can feel it. It's like you're emotionally pushing me away. And I don't understand. This whole fucking relationship is coming apart because I can't get you to open up. Give me *something* Harry.

Today, right now, at this minute, I don't know where the hell I stand. And when I ask you you don't seem to have an answer. You fumble for words or talk in circles. It can't go on any longer. I have to have answers. Even though it could mean the end of us, I'd rather have it over with than be suspended in this horrible emotional limbo. Do we continue to live together? Do we scrub the whole thing? Do we get married? It's come down to this: Are you ready for an honest commitment after four years, or not? Does this . . . this . . . whatever you want to call it, linger into infinity? Well, I'm sick and tired of being frozen out of your thoughts. I've tried to penetrate. I've asked questions. I've done the psychologist bit. I've explored all the avenues. And you still continue to hide behind this self-protective shield. Is it because of Ellen? Are you still laboring

5

under guilt for not helping her when she overdosed? Jesus. She was an impossible druggie that nobody could have saved. Is this it? Well, I don't intend to be a co-sufferer for your guilt and self-loathing. I've leaving. I need space. We both do. Maybe, when I'm gone, you'll sort it out. Hopefully this will be the case. I won't stop loving you, and I hate doing this, but if I continue like this, I'll wind up hating myself.

. . . there never will be complete equality until women themselves help to make laws and elect lawmakers.

—Susan B. Anthony

LAURIE

It is 10PM and Luaire is fed up with not being fed. Here she voices her frustration regarding her date's indecisiveness.

Look . . . I really don't give a damn. Chinese is fine. Italian is fine. German is fine. Russian is fine. Mexican is sensational. Sushi is wonderful. At this point, I don't give a fuck. Even a greasy hamburger would be beautiful. A double bacon-cheeseburger, blood-rare on a soggy bun—even this will do. Even though I never eat meat, haven't put meat in mouth for over four years, although I'm very strict in this department, even though the very thought of meat gives me diarrhea, I don't care. I'm so goddamned hungry I'm ready to eat the knobs off your car radio.

We've been driving around for over two hours. It's approaching ten o'clock. And I think it's about time you made up your mind where we're going to eat. We go in the Japanese place, you didn't like the look of the waitress—dirty fingernails. So, we get up and leave. Then we walk out of Roma Italiano because they seated us too close to the kitchen. Jesus, right now I wish I were *in* the kitchen. Then we drive all the way to Riverdale to the Chez Momarte. And here you really flip because the guy at the next table said there was fur in his rabbit. This is ridiculous. Besides, you didn't have to order rabbit. You could have ordered the *coq au vin* or the coquilles or the scallops. Or what about French fries? You can't go wrong with French fries in a French restaurant. And French fries are totally furless.

Then we drag all the way back to Roma Italiano where you get into a thing with the *maitre d'* because there's an hour wait. What the hell you expect, Goddammit? If we'd stayed put the first time, we'd be full of wine and pasta and belching our way to a movie instead of driving around in circles with our bellies kissing our spines.

Hey! Stop! Stop the car! Pull over! There's a McDonalds.

From a timid, shy girl I had become a woman of resolute character, who could no longer be frightened by the struggle with troubles.

—Ann Dostoevsky

JANET

Janet has insisted that Robert meet her for lunch. She knows it is time for a show-down, an honest discussion about the lack of sexual gratification between them.

We can't avoid it any longer. We have to talk. (*Beat.*) No. It can't wait. I'm tired of waiting. Every time I bring up the subject, you run from it. (*Beat.*) Yes, you do, dammit! You avoid it. Look . . . I know this isn't easy for you *or* me. But it's something that has to be discussed. (*Beat.*) Sorry . . . your work can wait. You can get back to the office late for once. You can't keep using your work as an excuse. You're always conveniently busy. But it won't work this time. I'm pining you down.

I don't know what's going on. Maybe it's four years. Maybe it's you. Maybe it's me. Maybe it's just the way it is. Maybe there isn't any answer. Sometimes these things are inexplicable and too deep for analysis.

In the beginning sex was great. Hell . . . we couldn't get enough. During the first year we were animals. Like the time we got it on in the kitchen while your parents were watching TV in the den. Jesus. The risks we took. But it was wild and reckless and fun. Wonderful! We were all over each other morning, noon, and night. I was so sore I walked like a cowboy. You had a perpetual hard-on, and I was wet as an eel. All you had to do was touch me and I was ready.

Then, little by little, the periods got further apart. Days, weeks . . . the last time was over two months ago. And I can't live with it. What ever happened to that beautiful erection? What ever happened to the wet and wild me? What was once a natural thing has become an obligation, a duty, a . . . Christ, the last time it was a chore. (*Beat.*) The hell it wasn't. There was no feeling in it—nothing. It was awful.

So, what are we going to do about it? (*Beat.*) Oh no. No way. Time's not the answer. That's a cop-out. We've got to get down to what's really going on here (*Beat.*) No. I'm not keeping my voice down. I'm not embarrassed. Fuck what people think. What do *you* think Robert? What do *you* feel?

So, we stop running, skirting the issue. We work it out, or we get out. I don't intend becoming a frustrated lay.

The extension of women's rights is the basic principle of all progress.

—Charles Fourier

SALLY

Sally holds back nothing in this trade against her greedy, un-caring sister.

Stop it! Stop it, goddammit! Enough! Jesus Christ, the woman's in there dying and you want to air old laundry. Even at a time like this you can't keep your fucking mouth shut. It's little wonder you can't keep a husband. Ever take time to figure out why you're a three-time loser? You think it was all Harold's and Robert's and Edward's fault? You ever try to put it in perspective? I don't think so. You're too busy with your own fucking narrow agenda, you're petty, small world of the everyday you.

Even now, with Mom fighting for her life in the next room, you insist on opening old wounds. Who cares who gets the farm, how we divide five hundred acres? Frankly, I don't give a fuck.

You come down here with Ralph, your little mealy-mouthed lawyer fuck, and make a big entrance and big stink and upset the whole the family. After more than three years living like an inflated, self-centered asshole in a high-rent condo in Manhattan, you descend on the farm like a fucking locust. Only difference is, locust fly away and you never see them again. You, you're a permanent pest.

So, you're concerned about the will, huh? Well, if I'm not mistaken, you can forget about inheritance. Mom left it all to Ray—everything. So, this leaves us both out. The difference is,

11

I don't care, I don't give a damn. Ray was here, on the scene, taking care of her day after day, cleaning up after her and caring. He deserves everything he gets, every cent, every acre, every single ounce of topsoil from fence to fence. Where the hell were you after she had her stroke? Why, hell, you didn't even have to common decency to send her a Christmas card, you money-grubbing, inconsiderate bitch.

My advise, big sister, is for you and your pin-stripped legal clown to pack up and clear the hell out. Now!

Where young boys plan for what they will achieve and attain, young girls plan for whom they will achieve and attain.

—Charlotte Perkins Gilman

DARLA

Darla, seriously emotionally damaged by her mother's callousness and being brutally molested by her father, rails on to her brothers in a state of hysteria. In her delirium, she imagines her former lover, Adrian, is on the scene. Adrian, however, is dead, killed nearly a year before in a motorcycle accident.

I'm a babe! Naked. A naked babe! Nothing more. A little girl with nothing, left on the doorstep of this here life! No one loves me. Never did. I was nothing. She hated me! Mom hated me! She's inside me! Growing. I'm full of her. I'm pregnant with my own mother. Help me, Adrian! Help me! (*Pulling her clothing from her body.*) Take me, Adrian! Take me in front of Mom and make her know I'm not a little kid no more, that I'm something, somebody she can't control any more! Oh, Jesus Christ in heaven, Adrian . . . take me! Take me! Christmas is special because it's a time to give. So, give me something that'll get her out of my life! Adrian, please! Please! (*Nearly nude, she stalks the set, running her hands along her body as if attempting to come to grips with her nightmares.*) You always made me feel little, Mom! Like I wasn't good enough! Like I was nothing! All I ever wanted was to be something, somebody. I tried, but you beat me down until I was nothing but a shadow of a person, something that nobody could even see. I hate you, you old bitch! And you, Dad, I hate you even more! For molesting me night after night. Me, your own daughter. Night after night I laid upstairs shivering because I knew what was coming. Night after night I held my breath till I was sick. You tore me apart, you bastard. You fucking no good drunken bastard. And she knew, oh yes, she knew. She could hear. She could hear me scream and cry and beg. But she never lifted a finger because it made her happy, because she got off on it. Sick goddamned bitch!

Can anything be more absurd than keeping women in a state of ignorance, and yet so vehemently to insist on their resisting temptation?

—Vicesimus Knox

KAREN

In the midst of a small-town council meeting, Karen rises and makes her plea for the defeat of pinball machines in the community.

It's gotta go! It's gotta go, I'm a tellin' ya! That there Lucifer's device has gotta go!

There's no place fer a devil's machine in a Christian community like this here. We got us standards t' keep. We got us kiddies t' raise clean an' pure in the shadow o' the cross! We don't act now, that there machine's gonna be the ruination of this here fine little place. We don't do somethin' right away, God only know what's-a gonna follow—gamblin, bettin', playin' the horses. God only knows! Once the devil gits a footholt he don't easy let go. Once he gets 'is horns in the youth-a this here community, once't they git the feel fer 'im, well . . . then that's gonna be the end o' peace an' security in our little town!

From little acorns mighty chestnuts grow. First pinball, then—*beer!* Then, heaven forbid—*a wet county!* Then, 'fore ya know it—*fast women!* Then Good-time men a comin' on down here lookin' fer wildness. No tellin' just where it'll lead to. An' think-a yer youth, those fresh little blossoms on the tree-a life. Think-a them. Think-a them a hangin' 'round down at that there ice cream store a pumpin' evey cent inta that there machine, spendin' their school money, money that should be a goin' fer books an' education, money they could be savin' up an' droppin' inta the collection plate of a Sunday as a way-a helpin' the work-a the Lord.

15

We gotta git that there pinball out now while the gittin's good! That there devil's machine with all them evil lights an' bells an' funny little demon balls! Damnation! Jesus drove the gamblers outta the temple. Now we gotta drive that there pinball outta this here county. We gotta rise up an' take holt before it's two machines an' then three and then . . . then who knows how many. The whole derned county'll be wall-t'-wall with slot machines an' pinballs an' gamblin' casinos an' sin! We gotta take up the Almighty sword an' cut out the cancer among us while the cuttin's good.

Praise the Lord!

I'm furious about Women's Liberationists. They keep getting up on soap-boxes and proclaming that women are brighter than men. That's true, but it should be kept very quiet or it ruins the whole racket.

—Anita Loos

BERTHA

In this speech, Bertha reinforces the bromide "A good man is hard to find."

I don't know. You don't know. *Nobody* knows. It's all a great big guessing game. You try to make the right choice, do the right thing, but there's no guidelines, no rules. You gotta play it as it happens. I know, I've tried it all, worked every angle, analyzed, tried to use good judgement. Know what? It's a crap shoot at best.

Like with James, for example. With him it looked like a perfect situation. Nice looking. Well-dressed. Good job with a big company. He had nice teeth, great hair, and an embossed calling card. Drove a new Mercedes. You look at a package like this and you just automatically assume when you unwrap it it's pure gold. Well, was I ever wrong. The man was solid lead. How was I to know he was a major, out-of-work, philandering asshole with a wife and three kids in Erie, Pennsylvania.

Then there was Herb, the stock broker. A very positive, authoritative person. I'd never met anyone as self-assured and impressive. Even his neckties looked important. He seemed to have all the answers. Gave me some great tips on the market. And he was charming, witty, had a great sense of humor. Which he needed when they hauled the crooked son of a bitch off to jail for stock fraud.

Larry was another case. We met at a Knicks game when I spilled mustard on his chinos. Most guys would have gone postal, but he was cool, didn't get crazy. It was almost like he was apologizing to *me*. He was the most laid-back person I'd ever met. Shy. Reserved. Frankly, I went nuts for the guy.

What woman wouldn't? He had this masculine inner-strength quality mixed with little-boy charm. When he smiled . . . forget it. We were a hot item for nearly six months before I found out he prefered the company of men.

There's just no way of knowing. I'm taking myself off the market for a while. Unless, maybe, I get introduced to someone by my mother. But even then, what the hell does she know? My dad left her last year for a twenty-one-year-old nympho he met at Hooters.

It is understood that the principles of the Declaration of Independence bear no relation to half of the human race.

—Harriet Martineau

FLORENCE

Florence surveys the aftermath of a Christmas party. The house is littered, broken mess. She is furious and vents her anger to her husband.

This is the last Christmas party. Just take a good look at this place. A disaster. A mess. Christ. It's one thing for people to be in the Holiday spirit, but when they're full of Holiday spirits they go bananas. Animals. A few Tom and Jerrys and the bastards don't have any respect for other peoples' property. *(Beat.)* Just having fun! Are you kidding. You call breaking the glass on the coffee table *fun?* You call spilling red wine on the sofa *fun?* You think throwing up on the carpet is *fun?* You won't think it's so goddamn funny when you get the bills. You have a pretty warped sense of a good time, if you ask me.

And what the hell was it with Frank Adams? Like all of a sudden he's a stand-up comic? Sober he's a cold, mealy-mouthed non-person. Then he comes here, has a few drinks, and alluva sudden he's doing standup. Jerk. He was a loud, insulting asshole who made everyone uncomfortable. And how about Juile? Was she wasted, or what? He boobs fell out twice. Merry Christmas huh? She should have painted one red and one green. *(Beat.)* What? Just having a good time? Typical male response. I wonder how you would have reacted if Don Simpson had pulled out his penis?

And the Brown-Hagens were the worst. Fucking phonies. They always come on so damned strong when we bump into them at the concerts. All ramrod-up–the-ass-straight-and-prissy, all-knowing with that phony-baloney accent. Butter won't melt in their arm pits. Then they come here, have a few drinks, and suddenly they're the Clampets. Fucking over-educated hillbillies. Why, did you ever hear such language out of a woman in your life? She's about as much Vassar as I am. When she fell into the coffee table, I wanted to kick her butt all the way back to Dogpatch. And he's worse. Him and that hundred-year-old blazer with that stupid crest. When I asked him what it signified, he couldn't tell me, he just belched and ate another hand-full of cashews.

Next year we do Christmas in Jamaica.

The most important thing women have to do is to stir up the zeal of women themselves.

—John Stuart Mill

CASSIE

Honesty is not always the best policy.

We were sitting at the bar at Cappuccino. He kept pushing me. He was relentless. He wouldn't stop pressing me about the night I took off and didn't come home till after five in the morning. We'd been through this a thousand times before. This is the reason I moved out, because he was always pumping me for details. But I never opened up. What person in their right mind would? But he never got over it. Even though we weren't living together anymore, he still had it in his craw.

We'd had dinner and things were going okay. Kind of catching up, you know, bringing each other up to date. But we'd each had a cocktail and we'd killed a bottle of wine. In other words, we weren't feeling any pain. And I shouldn't have been drinking at all. We all know how I am when I've had a few.

So, after dinner, we go to the bar for a brandy. Just what I needed—booze on top of booze, right? This is when he starts to pump me, and me, being half in the bag, didn't have sense enough to be discrete. And his questions didn't hold any anger, were more or less off-hand, you know, which fooled me completely. So, I start to open up.

I told him I'd left because I was fed up with his vacillating about his wife and family. After almost four years, he was still running back, spending his holidays and weekends with them. He just couldn't cut loose. After a while, no matter how much you care for a person, this wears thin. I felt like this non-person in the relationship—a whore. So, after he'd left that night I started in with the Grape Juice and Vodka and by midnight I was gone. Then I called Greg and he told me to come on over.

I spent the night with Greg doing dope and sex. I just didn't give a damn. It was my way of striking back, I guess. But I shouldn't have told Robert. He went crazy and slapped me right there at the bar in front of everyone. The bartender and owner stepped in and threatened to call the cops. When he calmed down a bit, they threw him out. This is the last I've heard of him. It's over. A bad ending.

The lesson I learned that night? Never, *never* tell.

No man, *not even a doctor, ever gives any other definition of what a nurse should be than this—'devoted and obedient." This definition would do just as well for a porter. It might even do for a horse. It would not do for a policeman.*

—Florence Nightingale

VOILET

Appointed to speak for her fellow workers, Violet lays it on the line to the company president regarding sex discrimination that is having a serious, negative impact on promotions and pay.

Look . . . I've come in here to have a reasonable discussion, okay? So, listen. For once, for you own good, for the good of the company—listen. And this isn't an idle threat. If necessary, we're prepared to back up our demands with action in the courts.

I want you to know I'm speaking for the more than three hundred women who work in this plant. They felt it would be a good idea for you and me to sit down and talk. Maybe this way you'll see the light and an we can avoid the necessity of a lengthy legal battle. Hopefully.

The sex discrimination in this shop has got to stop. Now. Immediately. (*Beat.*) C'mon, you know damned well what I'm talking about. We've been over it before. I'm talking about discrimination in promotions and pay. So, please, don't sit there and try to play it naïve. We're no longer going to stand idly by and put up with male domination. We're tired of being overlooked time and time again for raises and promotions. It's absolutely ridiculous. What the hell is this—the 1890s? Christ, working here is like a bad chapter out of Dickens. You know it and I know it, so let's not blow smoke, okay?

I'm more or less a typical example. I've worked hard for this company, done a good job for more than ten years. And I've been repeatedly passed over for promotions while the man working next to me, who isn't half the worker, gets promoted or a pay raise. (*Beat.*) What? Women fail the tests more than men? This is the most outrageous load of crap I've ever heard. Why the hell you think they fail? Because you don't to give them the special training, that's why. And you know it. It's deliberate. This way you legally avoid deserved promotions and pay raises.

Well, look, Mr. Profit Picture, you can sit there and deny all you want. You can posture and bullshit and hide behind technicalities. But while you're doing it, we're going to be in court suing your ass for fifty million.

Have a nice day.

Fighting is essentially a masculine idea; a woman's weapon is her tongue.
—Hermione Gingold

LINSAY

Linsay's sister, Darlene, has sacrificed her life for their domineering mother.

Sorry. (*Beat.*) Yes, I'm in a bad mood. How'd you guess? It's been a rough day. It isn't everyday I get up at four in the morning and fly twelve-hundred miles to be on hand for my mothers operation. You might say it's not your typical day. If you'd called me sooner, let me know what the hell was gong on, I could have been here helping out. (*Beat.*) C'mon. Frankly . . . that's bullshit. You've always, for some strange reason, kept me in the dark about her. What is it? Tell me. Resentment for me not taking more of the load? I thought we cleared the air on this years ago. You knew damned well I couldn't stay here. Not with Ralph and the kids and my job in Philadelphia. It would have been impossible. And you didn't have to become a martyr. Nobody asked you to sacrifice. This was your choice all the way. We even offered to pay her rent for a nice apartment after Dad died. But you insisted. Now I'm hearing something entirely different. Now, all of a sudden, you've been burdened, you don't have a life of your own, you've given up the best part of your life, you and Marvin would still be married if Mom hadn't moved in. Well . . . who the hell's fault is it, Darlene? Mine? Marvin's? Mom's?

If you remember, you took on the responsibility willingly. I fought against it. I told you it was mistake. You know how demanding she is. I don't know how Dad stood it all those years. No wonder he went to an early grave.

Look . . . we could have all chipped in and set her up independently and you could have gotten on with your life and marriage. But you just had to take care of her. You had to go the extra mile. Why? None of us could figure it out. Granted, it was a nice gesture, but at what expense? What was behind it? Guilt? Well . . . guilt doesn't work. It's a bad concept. And if you think the rest of us have to feel guilty, forget it.

The thing now it to figure out where she goes after she's released from the hospital. (*Beat.*) Nonsense. You're not giving up your life to an invalid. And she'll be worse than ever. She'll call every tune. You're going to get on with your life if I have to kidnap you and parachute you into Tibet.

O! men with sisters dear,
O! men with mothere and wives!
It's not the linen you're waring out,
But human creatures' lives!
　　　　　　　　　—Thomas Hood

ABBY

Her boyfriend is more than a committed paleontologist, he's obsessed. And Abby has had it!

I knew were a bone chaser. I knew this from the first. But I had no idea how hung-up you were on the subject. Well, this last trip to Montana told me all I need to know. Now I'm going to tell you what *you* need to know: You're not only a fucked-up bone freak, you're fucking obsessed.

I should have known better the first night I slept over and woke up looking at a poster of a T-Rex. This should have tipped me to something. But what did I know? Maybe it was a carryover from seeing *Jurassic Park* too many times, maybe you had a thing for "things." So, I figured, What the hell, nobody's perfect. Besides, you seemed like a sweet, harmless guy. The very least I could do was overlook your strange little hobby. But then, when you insist we go to the Royal Tyrell Museum of Paleontology in Alberta, Canada for our vacation, I'm getting the picture that maybe you're number one movie star is *King Kong.*

And then this last trip to Montana to study the ecosystem where they've found five tyrannosaurus skeletons. When you read about it, I swear I could see you getting an erection. What an over-reaction to a bunch of godamn bones.

So, off we go to Montana. You, me, and five thousand pounds of camping equipment crammed into a Ford Escort. And we drive through non-stop with you jabbering about how maybe dinosaurs were more scavengers than hunters. Like I really give a damn. For two days I hear this garbage and I'm wondering, How the fuck did I get myself hooked up with this nerd? And when we finally get there, you ignore me totally to concentrate on a well-preserved pelvis, nine articulated vertebrae, and a handful of ribs.

Well, good hunting, Edward. Maybe you'll stumble onto some more ribs in your back yard. As for me, I'll be looking for mine at Tony Roma's.

See you in three million years.

So this gentleman said a girl with brains ought to do something else with them besides think.

—Anita Loos

PAM

Pam was seated nearby when fellow workers were gunned down by a disgruntled ex-employee. Here, obviously shaken, she describes the incident to a reporter:

We only saw him occasionally. He worked in maintenance. He'd come into the office pool maybe six, seven times a year to replace lights or readjust the thermostat or make some minor repair. He was always very quiet. Didn't speak to anybody. He just did his thing and left.

It was just terrible. Terrible. The whole thing was just . . . it's beyond description really. Bizarre. Otherworldly. And it all happened so quickly, it seemed. In a flash. Here were are, doing our work, when, suddenly, he bursts in an starts shooting. There wasn't anything anyone could do. Besides, we were frozen with fear.

He went about the thing in this . . . this very rapid, but calculated and mechanical manner. This was the eerie thing, how calmly, methodically he did the killing. I think this is the part that sticks in my mind most vividly. It was like . . . like being suspended in a vacuum of terror witnessing this mass killing. And you were helpless—petrified.

And the killings certainly weren't random. He bypassed most of us during his rampage. First he killed two people in the reception area and then proceeded to kill others at their desks. He was picking and choosing. I've never felt such terror. Hell, maybe I was next. Who knew?

There was a tremendous amount of firepower. Three guns, at least. Maybe more. He was a walking arsenal, reloading as he went. It was a nightmare. The woman at the next desk,

Shirley Grimes, a mother of two beautiful children, was gunned down where she sat. Horrible. When he turned toward me, I was sure this was the end. But he passed me over. Why? Who knows? Who'll ever know the workings or a mind like that? It was a horrible, horrible thing.

If you educate a man you educate a person, but if you educate a woman you edicate a family.

—Ruby Manikan

SHELIA

Although Shelia has been married only a short time, her husband is pushing her to become pregnant. But she is unsure. She is ambivalent about child rearing, and also has serious apprehensions about pregnancy.

Yeah. He's pushing me. Already, after just six months, he wants a baby. And this wasn't part of the deal. We both agreed to wait, not put a timetable on it, you know. No pressure. But now, now it's a whole different story. He can't wait to be a father, he says. Can't wait to hold his son in his arms. As if it's going to be a boy. As if its sex is a given. I guess he thinks he can control this, too.

To be honest, Helen, I don't know if I'm ready for rug rats or not. I've never been a baby person. When we go see friends' babies I can't, for the life of me, find anything cute about them. For me they have no personality, all look like the Munchkins from the *Wizard of Oz*. Kids just aren't my thing. Harold knows this. He knew it going in. But now, all of a sudden . . . men, how the hell you figure? One minute it's romance and roses, the next you're a sperm receptacle.

I guess it's okay for me to give up a good job, a life, to become a slave to soaps and baby poop while Harold's out running around the country pretending to be a dot-com.

And how about being pregnant? This is no picnic, Helen. Who the hell needs it? Morning sickness. Weight gain. And you can forget about your wardrobe, honey. Sandy Hayes told me being pregnant was like carrying around two bags of groceries. Certainly something a man wouldn't know anything about. Said she had a perpetual aching back for six months. Six

31

months! I read recently where eighty percent of pregnant women have back pain—and often it doesn't end with delivery. Not very encouraging statistics.

Next time Harold brings up babies, I'm telling him Thanks a lot, but no thanks.

Every man who is high up likes to feel he has done it himself; and the wife smiles, and lets it go at that. It's our only joke. Every woman knows that.

—J. M. Barrie

VELMA

She refuses to succumb to motherly pressure.

The toilet won't stop running, the water pressure's so bad it takes you twenty minutes to shower, the refrigerator's noisy, the garbage disposal will only grind Jell-O, you got rats bigger than cats, giant bats, incessant gnats, killer bees in the attic, the roof leaks, the water is stagnant and crawling with disease, the electrical system is shot, your neighbors are ingrates, you found a Black Widow in your shoe, termites have established permanent residence in the walls, the plumbing's corroded, the floors are warped, the tile needs to be regrouted, the water heater is ready to blow, the air conditioning won't cool below eighty degrees, the heating system won't warm above sixty, every time you iron the lights dim, you're TV reception sucks, every morning there's pigeon shit on you car hood, the dog on your right craps on your peonies, the dog on your left barks from morning to night, rabbits eat your roses, there's noise pollution, air pollution, light pollution, radiation from power lines, you have prowlers, and the man behind you pees in the space between the garages. Holy Jesus Christ!

Mom! Is anything right? Is there one bright, tiny, little glimmer of light in your tragically fucked-up existence? Here you are, in the best neighborhood in the city in a beautiful $500,000 house. You have no debts. Your healthy as a horse. But, to hear you tell it, everything's going straight to hell. God. What next, the mailman's carrying the Ebola Virus?

This house is perfect. Dad left you in good shape. You've got it made and still . . . still all you do is bitch. This is bad. That's rotten. And not one of your complaints holds water. So, what's with you, anyway? As if I didn't know. But the answer again, for the zillionth time, is a definite *no*. You're *not* moving in with Bill and me. Out of the question. You're going to have to stay here and tough it out in your half-million-dollar lean-to.

Intimacies between women often go backwards, beginning in revelations and ending in small talk without loss of esteem.

—Elizabeth Bowen

TRISHA

Although they both care for each other, it appears their relationship is headed for the rocks due to incompatibility. Their frequent arguments, their ragging on each other, have placed them at the point of no return. Here Trisha confronts this. There is also the unresolved issue of Alan's lingering feelings for his former girl friend, Sandy.

If it goes on like this, we'll have to separate. (*Beat.*) Yes. (*Beat.*) No. I'm not kidding. (*Beat.*) But I've heard this before. You've heard it before. I'm as guilty as you are. But it seems, no matter how hard we try, we can't make it work. For some reason, we snap at each other for the smallest things, insignificant things that don't mean a damn. And the sad thing of it is, we care for each other. (*Beat.*) I don't know. I can't answer that. Maybe we should give it a month. Two. Maybe six. I don't know. I don't have a pat answer. (*Beat.*) I know it's radical, but we can't go on eating each other alive over every silly goddamn issue.

Look, I don't know if it's my insecurity or ego or what the hell it is. Or your insecurity or ego. All I know is, we can't go on being at each other's throats. What kind of a life is that? And then, whether you like to admit it or not, there's the overidding issue of Sandy. (*Beat.*) Like hell it isn't. It's a major problem, Alan. (*Beat.*) Bullshit. Face it, you've never gotten over her. (*Beat.*) Like hell. Then how come you're always comparing me to her? (*Beat.*) Yes, you do. How you think this makes me feel?

Alan, stop being so goddamned defensive. Face reality here. You have any idea how often you bring her up? (*Beat.*) What?

35

I can't believe this. Jesus. Talk about denial. No wonder we're having problems. (*Beat.*) So the sex is good, so what? This isn't enough. There has to be more.

Come to think of it, I take back the part about my insecurity and ego. What woman in her right mind wouldn't be a bitch on wheels when the man she's living with is still hung up on his former lover?

On second thought . . . let's make the separation a year.

Do you know why God witheld the sense of humor from women? That we may love you instead of laughing at you.

—Mrs. Patrick Campbell

JANICE

Just having completed a job interview, Janice rejects the position, admonishes the personnel director for his misogynistic questions and attitude of male superiority.

(*Waving her job application.*) I'm sorry if it doesn't meet your definition of "wholesome." I could have lied, written some fiction about how pure my life has been. But I'm not that desperate for work. I wonder how many applications you get that are truthful? Very damned few, I'll bet on it. Because a lot women will go to any lengths to be "womanly." And do you know why? I'll tell you why: Because it's men like you who threaten them and put them in this position. Still, unfortunately, there are still enough misogynist pigs like you around to intimidate women who are vulnerable and needy and not in a position to stand up for their respect and dignity. Well, Mr. Personnel . . . I'm not one of these women. And I don't intend to be—ever.

The job you offer is damned attractive. Good pay, benefits. And the hours are flexible. This is what attracted me—the hours. Because I'm a single mother who has to work around her childrens' schedule. So, what you offered sounded ideal. But, after spending a few minutes here, listening to your questions, having you talk down to me like I'm some infant, I wouldn't work for this company if you gave it to me.

How does a man like you ever become head of personnel? Obviously because you reflect the values of the people who run the joint. Reactionary, prejudiced people, people unable to move with the times and embrace human values. It's a fucking shame people like you sit in judgement of anyone, especially women.

Here's what I think of your job. (*She takes the application and rips it in two, dumps it on his desktop.*) There! Ripped in half it'll be much easier to shove you-know-where. Good luck with your next interview. I'm sure you'll find someone who will agree with your points of view. Problem is, how will you know they're not lying?

It is only the women whose eyes have been washed clear with tears who get the broad vision that makes them little sisters to all the world.

—Dorothy Dix

LUCINDA

She is not certain she wants a breast implant. Although flat-chested, she fears the operation and its results. But her boyfriend is urging her to proceed. Here she expresses her reservations to a friend:

I don't know, Elise, maybe it's no big deal. But, still, they have to cut and . . . I'm not crazy about people hacking on me, you know. (*Beat.*) That's easy for you to say. You're an altogether different type. Fearless. You've always been a risk taker. But I'm just not that way. Never have been. You know how I am. I've been this way since I was a kid. I think it comes from an over-protective mother. You know, the "Don't go to close to the edge, don't run with scissors" type.

On the other hand, I hate being flat as a airstrip. Sometimes, when I stand in front of the mirror, I see this young boy looking back at me. It's no wonder Jim wants me to go ahead with the implant. And I guess this is as good a reason as any. I mean, if your boyfriend's turned off. But, then, this is nonsense, too. I mean, what you see is what you get, right? I was flat-chested when we met, wasn't I? So, why now, all of a sudden, are big boobs such a major thing? As if after I'll be a different person. Under the false front I'll still be the same old building.

(*Beat.*) You think? I don't know if I'll feel better about myself or not. And what if the operation is a debacle? Look what happened to Esther Woodhouse. Her guy screwed up bad. Poor thing. She's a mess. Has to go in for a retread. She showed them to me. Scary. Different sizes. One droops, the other makes a left turn. I know this Dr. Eddington is supposed to be the best in the tits department, but anyone can have an off day, you know.

I just not sure. And this thing with Jim pisses me off. You'd think if he really loved me, the size of my breasts wouldn't be an issue. Weasel. Think I'll make a bargain with him. If he has a penis enlargement, I'll consider the boob job.

If women didn't exist, all the money in the world would have no meaning.
—Aristotle Onassis

JASMINE

Well along in her pregnancy, Jasmine has serious trepidations about an abortion at this stage. She also feels her moral obligation outweighs expediency. Her husband, initially supportive, is now against having the child, does not want to take on the responsibility.

You're not making this any easier, you know. When I mention keeping the baby you go ape. Where the hell were you six months ago? Then it was neat, it was exciting, it would be wonderful being a father. Then I still had time. It was early. Even though it was still one helluva moral decision, it was a lot less complicated. But you were so damned enthusiastic. So, I delayed. I procrastinated. I was going through all kinds of indecision and you knew it. I really didn't want a child. Had it not been for your enthusiasm, I probably would have gotten rid of it. Immediately.

Now, as far as I'm concerned, I'm way past the point of no return. And now you've done a one-eighty. Once you were gung ho, now a child's an added responsibility, an added expense. What? Why the big turnaround? It's not going to be any more expensive now than it was six months ago. And now, here I am in the third trimester. And I'm not about to go getting rid of a child at this stage. Jesus. It'd be sick as hell.

You realize how far along I am? This isn't just some fetal blob I'm carrying around anymore, this is a *baby,* Mark! A fully-formed, living thing. Look, I've seen pictures of abortions at this stage. Not a pretty sight, let me tell you. It's downright gross. They take them and . . . I won't go into details.

What's got me going bananas here is you're no longer supportive. Here I am, big as a goddamn balloon, and I've got a husband whose main concern is his bank account. Hey! What about taking responsibility?

Look, I'm having this baby. So, get over it, okay? And when the baby's born, accept it and give it love. Something I need a lot of right now.

Most good women are hidden treasures who are only safe because nobody looks for them.

—Dorothy Parker

ROBERTA

Noble Johnson, Roberta's elderly, bachelor neighbor, has just told her his bittersweet story of unrequited love and how he has avoided attending his high-school reunions for fear of running into his one-and-only love. Here Roberta attempts to alter his thinking:

Mr. Johnson—Noble—I think you're making a terrible mistake. (*He attempts to interrupt, but she stops him with a raised hand.*) Please . . . let me finish.

Look, I know it's none of my business, I know I'm probably way off base here, but, even at the risk of upsetting you, I've got to tell you what I think, okay? This business of avoiding seeing Amy is not healthy. In fact, it only makes matters worse. You just can't go on living with this inside you, avoiding reality for the rest of you life. You're losing too much. Look how much you've lost already. Here you are, a healthy, good-looking man sitting around inside of memories, bound up in the past, reliving something that happened forty-some years ago.

I loved your story. It was beautiful, touching. But it's also damned sad. Especially sad for you, because you're trapped in it like some tragic character. And now you have a chance, maybe a last chance, to see Amy and talk and reminisce and relive all those happy moments, and you're throwing it all away, going to blow it because you're afraid. Or, and please excuse me for saying this, you're just plain stubborn and full of pride. But what does your stubbornness and pride get you? Nothing. Nothing but loneliness and self-pity. And this is really very sad.

Whatever the reason—fear, stubbornness, pride—whatever, you should put it all aside and go to this reunion, because seeing her will be a healing thing. Believe me. It'll be a way of coming to grips, getting things behind you, facing up, putting the past to rest.

Do you not know I am a woman?
When I think, I must speak.
            —William Shakespeare

AMY

Amy and William, who haven't seen each other since high school, have a chance meeting. A once dowdy, over-weight intellectual, Amy has transformed herself emotionally as well as physically. Here she brings William up to date about herself:

During the summer, right after getting out of high school, I was pretty much a stay-at-home. Did a lot of reading. Reading was always my way of avoiding people, avoiding the fact I was unpopular, not facing up to my weight problem. I always had an armload of books with me, remember? I lived inside books back then—fantasized. I remember how I would have died to have been Daisy in *The Great Gatsby*.

I fancied myself this intellectual who knew more than anybody. You talk about your self-delusion. What it really was, I was ashamed of my weight and, for that reason, I hid behind my smarts, stayed away from people—especially boys. I only dated a few times in high school. Billy Creamer. Remember him? The real skinny kid with the thick glasses who looked like he was in pain all the time? (*She chuckles at the remembrance.*) God, he was even more bookish that I was. The few times we went out we sat in his car and discussed Shakespeare's sonnets. This was as sexy as it got.

Anyway, this is the way I was till about midway through my sophomore year in college. Then, one day, while trying to squeeze my size fourteen body into a size eight, I decided enough was enough. So, I went on a diet of no chocolate, more vegetables, and less intellect. And I started exercising. With getting thinner and not working at being an intellectual boor came self-esteem, more dates and a hell of a lot more fun.

Looking back now . . . (*She shudders at the memory.*) ugh. I was a mess.

I'm one of the lucky ones, I guess. I finally saw the light and did something about it. It's damned hard looking at yourself, you know.

Frailty, thy name is woman!
 —William Shakespeare

KATHY

Her name is Kathy McKinnon, but to her many fans she's Lancer, an internationally-known professional wrestler. Here, fed up, she tells her boyfriend he'll have to get over his insecurities and petty jealousies because of her fame and high-profile profession:

No, I'm not giving it up. Are you kidding? Are you nuts? Why should I give up a highly lucrative profession that I love because of your childish insecurities, because what I do threatens you in some crazy way, because you're jealous? Well, insecurity, paranoia, jealousy, a domineering mother, bad potty training . . . whatever, get over it. You think I've worked this hard and long to throw it all away because of your childishness? Forget it.

Look, I've taken hard knocks all my life. I've had to struggle and overcome more shit than you can ever imagine. Just coping with growing up with five older brothers was a lesson in survival. I had to fight for every inch of territory. And my father was a cruel, drunken sonofabitch who had this thing for women. Misogynist bastard. You can't imagine what life was like for me and my mom in that household. Place was nothing but a male training ground for future insensitive brutes. My dad saw to it my brothers were screwed-up from the beginning. He went out of his way to make certain they'd grow up to be macho assholes. I haven't spoken to any of them in years.

I got the hell out of Altoona right after high school. Went to Penn State on an athletic scholarship. My specialty was the hurdles and relay. Also a lot of contact stuff. Mixing it up never bothered me. So, when I got a shot at the WWF it was right down my alley. I was a natural. And it was my ticket to a future. Because of it, I'm well-known, rich, and I can afford to keep my mother in a nice apartment in Pittsburgh.

So, why would I want to give it all up. For a lover? (*Laughs.*) Hey! Lovers are easy. Life is hard.

God made woman for the man,
And for the good and increase of the world.
 —Alfred, Lord Tennyson

KITTY

A former druggie speaks out at AA:

My name is Kitty, and I'm not an alcoholic. My problem is drugs. It started when I was a teenager. Seemed like drugs were easier to get then than alcohol was. Well . . . easier because a kid in the neighborhood, this rich kid, had access to everything—meth, crack, cocaine, heroin—you name it.

Maybe our problem was we had too much money. This and way too much time on our hands. None of us, the kids in my neighborhood, had to worry about anything. We lived in the most upscale section of Chicago. We had it made. We had cars, clothes—everything. We were all in private schools.

The guy I was talking about—we'll call him Jeff—was into drugs before anybody. And, because he had dough, he used to go down to the South Side and buy. I went with him a couple of times. A terrible place. It looked like a war zone, you know. Trash all over the place, old, rusted-out cars, people milling around aimlessly. It was a pretty intimidating atmosphere, let me tell you.

But Jeff knew his way around down there. And this is where he had his connection. He'd carry his money in his knapsack. He made his buys in this old, dilapidated building. On the second floor. He'd go up to this door and knock and a guy would appear from behind a little opening in it. Couldn't really see his face. Jeff'd shove the money through the hole and the guy would shove out the coke—whatever.

It all seemed so innocent. We'd get together. Friends from school and a couple of neighborhood kids. At Jeff's house. His parents were gone a lot, so we had the place to ourselves. We'd turn on and have sex and . . . well, you know.

My habit just escalated. You think it's fun. You don't see the problem. I mean . . . what the hell, you know. And then, then you can't live without it and you lose all perspective and you'll do anything to get it.

The morning they dug me out of rat hole, after I'd almost OD'd, this was the turning point. Now I think I'm going to make it. One day at a time.

I've got a woman's ability to stick to a job and get on with it when everyone else walks off and leaves it.

—Martgaret Thatcher

ELEANOR

After an absence of many years, Eleanor recently returned to her home town where she has been residing with her sister. She has always been a free spirit, a bit of a hell raiser, the black sheep of the family. Her return has created conflicts, resulting in her decision to leave. Here she expresses to her sister her feelings about their relationship, the narrow attitudes still prevailing in this rural, provincial area. She is packing as she speaks:

I hate this goddamned town. The people. Do they ever change? They haven't the slightest clue what's going on in the world. Their narrow attitudes. Unbelievable. Do they have any idea about anything? And you've become just like them. Narrow. Critical. Judgmental. It's a goddamn fucking shame. My own sister slipping into this.

How many years? Fifteen? And I come back to the same picture. Just like when I left. Like it was painted yesterday. The picture's still wet!

I should have known better. I should have stayed away. But, what the hell, you're all I have left. We're all *we* have left. But it was a mistake. Because in this town they don't allow for error. So, I've been nothing but trouble for you. An embarrassment. You think I don't see how people look at me? And I'm sure they gossip. "There goes Eleanor Payne, Helen's evil sister. Married three times. Alcoholic. Can't settle in one place." Like it's any of their fucking business.

I try my best, you know. Okay, so I have hang-ups. This is no secret to me. Look . . . at least I'm coping, I'm still above ground. And, coming back here, I figured maybe I'd be able to get some tranquility in my life. Maybe reconnect. Get some understanding and love.

You know, Helen, as fucked-up as I might be, I'm a hell of a lot better off than you. Coming back here really opened me up to the fact that—with all my problems—I'm much better off than you and the narrow-minded people in this yesterday's pit hole.

I would venture to guess that Anon, who wrote so many poems without signing them, was often a woman.

—Virginia Wolf

ZELDA

Zelda eschews the exercise/diet scene, questions the "benefits."

I'll tell you this, I'm not about to go walking and running and buying treadmills. I'm not joining health clubs and spas and gyms. I'm not buying into aerobics. No special diets. This is for the dedicated, the committed, the involved. Well, I'm none of the above. Never have been. You've known me for years. When's the last time you heard me order a riceburger, veggieburger or watercress milkshake? I've never been into self-improvement. I've always been into self-indulgence.

If I were this soggy bag of dreck, maybe I'd consider some moderate form of exercise. Like gin rummy. But I feel good and look decent and I'm not overweight. How? Who knows? Good genes? Luck? I haven't a clue. And I'm not questioning. I think it's bad Karma to question good health.

I've given some thought to your suggestions. But I just can't bring myself to wearing spandex and eating vitamins.

You know, Nancy, I'm the only person I know who doesn't own a pair of those horrible looking athletic shoes. And I don't carry a bottle of some-kind-or-other liquid around with me. You, on the other hand, would drink Evian under water. I don't understand it, have no relationship to it. Back in West Virginia, where I grew up, people only drank water with dinner. If they didn't have beer, that is. And the only people who ran had a police car behind them.

I'm not saying exercise and diet isn't good. It's just not for me, that's all. Maybe I'll pay for it later, I don't know. Or maybe you will. Who says all this jumping and bending and stretching isn't going to backfire? Hell, you're already living on Advil. You've always got injuries. Bad back. Knees hurt. Today you can't raise your arm because it hurts your shoulder. You're in such good shape you can hardly move.

Maybe you should hang in tonight. Give it a rest. There's a neat old movie on AMC. I'll open a bag of Cheese Curls.

Women have served all these centuries as looking-glasses possessing the magic and delicious power of reflecting the figure of man at twice its natural size.

—Vigrinia Wolf

CLAUDIA

Claudia knows full well the consequences of smoking, and is
determined that her lover give up the filthy habit.

Why do I want you to stop? Why do I want you to stop? What
a ridiculous question. Isn't it fairly obvious? You mean, you
don't have a clue here? Please. Look, I'm not telling you how
to live your life. Your life is your business. But your life plus
me is *our* business. You wanna exclude me, you do what the
hell you want. But I'm here, I'm on the scene. In case you
haven't noticed, it's me sitting on the other side of the *Times*
every morning.

Look, cigarettes killed my dad. They killed my aunt. My
best friend, back in Cleveland, very talented . . . dead at thirty
because she couldn't keep two packs a day of Marlboros out of
her lungs. Get the picture? It's a lousy, killing habit, Sean. And
you ask why I want you to stop. Because I give a damn, that's
why. Because I love you. Is this too far out, to convoluted for
you to absorb? I would think not.

For over a year you've been promising to quit, and the best
you've done is switch brands to some "safe" smoke. Christ.
You and I both know this is bullshit. I don't care how they
pack it or filter it or treat it, it's still lethal. Hour by hour your
sucking death into your body. And that little thing between
your fingers is calling the tune. You're a goddamned slave to
it. First thing in the morning. Last thing at night. Running
outside every few minutes to be with your little white mistress.

You can't keep this up. It's crazy. And it's making me
crazy. And it's all so fucking stupid and silly and wasteful.
And I'm not going to sit around while you smoke yourself into

a funeral and say nothing and do nothing. And this time I mean it. It's got to stop. You get help. The patch. Therapy. Will power. I really don't give a damn what. But your killing addiction has got to come to a noisy halt. You can lean on me. I'm here. We'll beat it together.

What we have here is special. And I want it to continue. I don't want you inhaling away our future.

From women's eyes this doctrine I derive:
They sparkle still the right Promethean fire;
They are the books, the arts, the academes,
That show, contain, and nourish all the world.
                                    —William Shakespeare

JENNIFER

She's a sensuous, desirable woman with strong, womanly desires who, after weeks of physical rejection, has decided to call it quits.

Yes, Mary, I understand. But Jim just can't be this naïve. I don't care what you say, no man his age can be this sexually retarded. Where the hell has the guy been all his life, sealed up in Tupperware? Nobody can be this innocent. And even though he's handsome, it still isn't enough. No woman gets a climax from a profile. Face it, the man's a sexual invalid. He should put his dick in a cast, it's broken, it doesn't work, and, at his age, it's out of warranty. And why, because he's screwed up in the head, that's why.

Everyone knows the penis starts in the brain. Freud proved this in the last millennium. A man's dick is between his ears. It's a mental trip all the way. If the guy's got emotional hang-ups the brain says, "Sorry, Mr. Penis, but standing at attention is out of the question." The mind calls the shots. And when the mind tells it to be limp, what have you got? Soggy pepperoni.

At first, I thought he was being gentlemanly. Didn't even kiss me on our first date. Or the second. The third. Finally, on the fourth, he gave me a peck on the cheek. After six months, we'd gotten down to some light petting. But, by this time, I'm past light petting and ready for heavy groping. So, I figure, this is a problem requiring drastic measures. So, I suggest we go to Santa Barbara for the weekend. A nice romantic spot near the ocean. He agreed, so I figured he was ready to unleash that devil between his legs.

We get a nice room, okay? Right on the beach. Ocean's lapping at our door. Perfect. We hang out, swim, dress, have a nice candlelight dinner. When we get back to our room, I go in the bathroom, strip down to my garterbelt and come out expecting to see that lovely frankfurter. But no hotdog. Jim had taken a separate room.

I haven't seen the jerk since. The hell with him. I haven't got time for him to figure out his problem. After six months on the wagon, I've got my own. This afternoon I'm attacking my pool man.

The average man is more interested in a woman who is interested in him than he is in a woman—any woman—with beautiful legs.

—Marlene Dietrich